Maps *for* Migrants *and* Ghosts

CRAB ORCHARD SERIES IN POETRY
OPEN COMPETITION AWARD

Maps *for* Migrants
and Ghosts

LUISA A. IGLORIA

Crab Orchard Review &
Southern Illinois University Press | Carbondale

Southern Illinois University Press
www.siupress.com

23 22 21 20   4 3 2 1

Cover illustration: *Juan Tamad Series*, by Santiago Bose (2000), courtesy of
Lilledeshan Bose and the estate of Santiago Bose

The Crab Orchard Series in Poetry is a joint publishing venture of Southern
Illinois University Press and *Crab Orchard Review*. This series has been made
possible by the generous support of the Office of the President of Southern
Illinois University and the Office of the Vice Chancellor for Academic
Affairs and Provost at Southern Illinois University Carbondale.

Editor of the Crab Orchard Series in Poetry: Jon Tribble
Judge for the 2019 Open Competition Award: Allison Joseph

Library of Congress Cataloging-in-Publication Data
Names: Igloria, Luisa A., [date] author.
Title: Maps for migrants and ghosts / Luisa A. Igloria.
Description: Carbondale : Southern Illinois University Press, [2020] |
Series: Crab orchard series in poetry
Identifiers: LCCN 2019059622 (print) | LCCN 2019059623 (ebook) |
ISBN 9780809337927 (paperback) | ISBN 9780809337934 (ebook)
Subjects: LCGFT: Poetry.
Classification: LCC PS3553.A686 M37 2020 (print) |
LCC PS3553.A686 (ebook) | DDC 811/.54—dc23
LC record available at https://lccn.loc.gov/2019059622
LC ebook record available at https://lccn.loc.gov/2019059623

For Oliver

Who other than you will ask for news of me?
—Arundhati Roy, *The Ministry of Utmost Happiness*

KHARON: *Take the oar and push her to. Now pay your fare and go.*

—Aristophanes, *The Frogs*

CONTENTS

III

I

Song of Meridians

It's spring, but in other places it's not-
        yet-spring. It's dry, or wet with

monsoon, or it is why-is-there-still-snow-
        on-the-ground. It's strange and high,

that mechanical whine in the night, coming
        from somewhere beyond the ceiling.

It's Wednesday, and in another place already
        Thursday; it's night, though here it is

still half past noon. And look at the news-
        paper: on the upper left, a woman in a pale

peach dress is smiling and waving her hand.
        On the bottom right, there's a picture

of cities burning: it's spring, or whatever
        season it is for laughter or slaughter, a

difference of one letter between one state
        of being and another. It's that time when cows

and sheep are calving, when blood is the marker
        for a life breaking away, or maybe just breaking.

The Heart's Every Heave

Say cotton, say the crease
in the sleeve of a shirt,

the plainness in a collar,
the brim of a hat. If the future

is here, whose face greets you
in the mirror as you collect

water in your hands; as you hand
your money over the counter

to pay for bread, a cup of coffee,
a ticket? A man on the train steps

in the path of someone he doesn't
even know, or trails another man

home in his truck for two
whole miles to spew insults

in his foreign-looking face. How
is this the future too? Your heart

holds its breath, lurches from platform
to crowded lobby. Say elegy, insistence,

not blank stare. Say danger and defiance.
Not shoulder shrug, not fold over.

Fatalism

~ *after "El Flautista" ("The Flutist"), Remedios Varo; 1955*

A cardinal touches down on a Japanese maple
but can't tell us where they've taken

all the children. We take turns watching,
we take turns playing songs for the mothers:

their grief, our grief, might merge
to form a thing that could unseal a stone

from the mountain. Only there is no one
walking out into the light as if resurrected.

That copper-tinged wind, that citadel
whose once beautiful blueprint is fading.

The light, too, is dismantling; or in the throes
of change. My face is the inside of a shell up-

turned to the moon. A rune, a coelacanth.
Night-blooming cereus stranded in time.

Maps for Migrants and Ghosts

"Ask me where I'm from, & . . . / I may point at the dirt
as if it were the embodiment of all things."
> ~ James A. H. White, "[Im]migratory Patterns"

Are there little fish swimming in jars of brine
in the cupboard, are there pickled moons and stars,

curtains of smoke after a fireworks festival
when dancers ripple into the streets to show off

their ink? In that other world, we wait for tinny
bell-chime and scrape of foot pedal, the call

of the scissors-grinder widening through sleepy
towns. Heat rising from the heads of schoolchildren

at three in the afternoon, yeasty like bread. The stronger
the scent, the better. Even the gods and ancestors

should thrive in other places, though they don't understand
the need for gendered pronouns. They resent filling out

forms which could be used to make claims for erasing
their existence: O pity you poor collectors

of blunt throwaway instruments. Penitents inch toward
the river, the expert *thwack* of bamboo whips calling forth

the blood. There are questions that could never
be answered. Like stars, at the heart of every place

a central note is buried: say anise, say achuete
oil, say hair singed off the belly of a thrashing pig.

Casida of Weeping

~ after Lorca

Dear Federico, it is impossible
to shut all the balconies of the world
to the sounds of weeping. The angels
were arrested as they crossed

the border, their wings torn off
and crumpled into sheets of tinfoil.
It is impossible to describe
the tears of the separated

though their weeping has been
recorded. In the distance, dogs
and sentinels limp from one
mile marker to another,

exhausted. And dear Federico,
a mother could not ever forget you.
Or a father. Or a grandfather.
Their cries make the sound

of hundreds of strings pitched
to sundering. Like you, all we hear
pouring over the balconies
is the sound of weeping.

Moving, Changing, Not Moving

In the brick-lined interior of a coffee shop, a man
at the communal table closes his eyes, a pair

of earphones plugged into his cell. Fanning themselves,
people come in from the street; it's the hottest summer

& everyone wants iced coffees & teas, water &
ice; & parents with little children fall in line outside

gender-neutral bathrooms. How long has he sat like that?
How long will he stay? One of my daughters went

on a date recently to a nearby botanical garden, but the corpse
flower they'd wanted to see had already opened. Not even

its decline was left to observe—its burgundy-lined spathe
now just a wilted sac, a gathered & pleated skirt around

the spadix. *Let nothing disturb you, Let nothing frighten you,*
All things are passing away, said the saint who swooned

back into a billowing cloud as if it were a fainting couch.
O my heart, still so slow at learning to walk the perimeter

of dying: the motionless man, the Saturday crowd, the in-
florescence marked with the stench of rotten meat & putrid

cheese, sweaty socks & sweet-heavy ammonia; the sudden
downpour that brings a haze of petrichor up from dry soil.

Photograph, 1959

Depending on the slant of light,
      time shifts the delineation of the day:

and truth is tinted amber-grey, mauve,
      warm honey; or sepia darkened at softly

crumpled edges. She looks out at you:
      still-young eyes beneath a beehive

hairdo; pale, pink-lipsticked smile. It is
      sometime in November, in a stuffy booth

at La Suerte photo studio. A photographer
      has raised his arm and counted backward—

three-two-one—as though right there,
      the world were on the cusp, about to crown

out of the camera's velvet drape. The angle
      of her head, the modest neckline, contrivance

of flowers and a scroll-backed chair complete
      this portrait of her pulchritude. Where are we

at this point in history? Not quite embodied
      flesh nor bone, nor calcium littered among

the stars. No, nor scheme to capture destiny—
      On the reverse side of the print, just a signature's

watery flourish, addressing what's to come.

Coup de Grâce

She has recurrent dreams of a hot fire licking at her hands and feet, drawing her into its center. She sees her dead sister there, her dead husband, motioning for her to cross over. She is by turns ecstatic and furious. She moans and cries, then bellows like a bull provoked for the matador. She likes the blazing red cape, the suit of lights edged with gold; but not so much the lances. For all these visitations, her body *has not given up the ghost.* What does this mean, anyway? Whose ghost lives in her, spurring bouts of energy, hunger for fruit, for bread, roast meat; the mean anger, the need for control? Whatever it is, when she's in pain she prays for it to be swift—A wisp of smoke from a snuffed candle. A tug in both directions, so the gold chain breaks.

Mother: Three Pictures

She is beautiful in that photograph where they are dancing in a roomful of other couples. She has a beauty mole penciled on her cheek, slightly to the right of her lip. Her eyebrows are two perfect arches, her hair a dark beehive. I think there are dots on her dress. Where is this photograph? I would like very much to have it.

*

In another she is posing on a terrace overlooking the crater lake with Taal Volcano in the center. She is beside a famous painter who has nonetheless been introduced to us as *the wife of a famous painter*: a long-lost cousin of my father who paints in the naïf style—audacious colors, bold outlines. You could say that piety is her subject: all saints, religious icons. Mother looks like a young Audrey Hepburn with a cropped hairstyle, in a plain black dress she sewed herself.

*

I vaguely remember seeing a thin album of wedding pictures, all in sepia. I do not think she wore a veil. Her dress may have been a sheath. There was a picture of them cutting a cake. From the church ceremony, a picture of father's niece and nephew putting the cord around their shoulders. The cord like an 8. Infinity grounded by a knot in the center.

We don't live in the light

only to forget everything;
    neither do we lie in the dark
just to barter these days
of bee hum and wheatgrass

for a mouthful of seeds—
    When the days are long like this,
        the heart casts a longer shadow;
    the future swings like a bell
or flaps like a shirt or shroud

drying to a certain shape
    on the line—I count out
        the hard clicking of abacus
            beads to clear more space;
    but the hours hurtle toward

their edge. Am I supposed
to become that woman then,
    crazed by the blinding silence
        of snow, seduced by the river's
            mystery under ice? When I keen

        into the wind, door hinges rattle
    as if possessed—I won't quiet them.
Once I was a body that housed
    other bodies. I was expected
        only to give, not to take—

Once I was told to seal
one mouth and open the other.

Self-Portrait, with Beetles in Sugar

Summer almost gone
and the fruit abundant
but still green and hard
on the tree, I rejoiced
one morning at the sight
of something deep-colored
and gleaming on a high
branch:
                    but the clusters
turned out to be Japanese
beetles, helmeted in khaki
green; drunk on sugar,
burrowed deep in the hips
of a ripe fig, its skirts flayed
open in the shimmering
heat.
              I stepped back, stunned
at how stunned this scene
rendered me; then rapidly
dismayed by the threat
of more widespread
invasion—the idea
of things seething up,
chthonic, from some
underworld.
                    I could find
a ladder, don gloves and
peel them off one by one
from the leaves to drown
in a bucket of water—
but not before remembering
what it was like to myself
be taken:

to have thought
in my confusion this
was fate, or simply
the natural order
of things.

Measure

At my wrist, constant beat of what the gecko sings in the eaves:
    Be brave, be brave. I try to quiet that pulse when it hammers

too loud in my ears, when the merest tender bar of moonlight
    threatens to break a dam of pent-up tears. In the mountains,

many years ago, I dreamed I could give myself to a lifetime
    of work and words. And this morning I knew when a bird

touched down in the fig by the tremble in the net of leaves.
    What it tells me is that the unseen magician has pulled

almost all the knotted silk squares from out of his sleeves—
    rippling blue, golden yellow, crimson visible from miles away.

When I move to the couch to lie down in afternoon heat, I feel
    his very fingertips press down on my lids. These days,

I am either sad and angry, or bitter and sad. I'm begging,
    don't let these be the only combinations at the end.

Hibernal

So long now has that story of deep wintering
        obsessed me: how the club-footed god sets his sights,

plucks a girl out of a field as easily
        as a flower, takes her down with him.

Which is to say, look beyond the metaphor of brute
        abduction to the underworld. But for the most part,

this has been the mother's story—how she scours
        the land and badgers the powers that be to get her back.

Fallow the fields and seas; famine and drought,
        fruitlessness, the icy blade of her anger raking

across the countryside—I've wished too
        for that wide level of influence but mine

doesn't extend as far. Season after season
        I work but brace myself for another

failure to raise ransom for permanent
        parole. Season after season, stoic, I keep

clean and stark the banner of my hope:
        bone buried in a field of snow.

Theory of Instruction

The light, and the flower inside it; its flickering,
   its gradual fading. Trickle of sand in a glass crucible

correcting itself, spelling out time. Everywhere
   there are streets named after saints or dead

dictators—in this way we are reminded every memory
   can negotiate its price. Don't we already have fables

that try to pass for facts? In blue cages on the patio,
   children chirp lessons until the curator comes to spread

a gray drop cloth. In college, my art professor
   pointed to a slide of St. Theresa, the angel's lance

poised above the flesh of her breast. Isn't that how we
   look in the throes of falling or flying? I was taught

suffering is another name for holy. I was told to distrust
   the beautiful flames of pleasure that sing like birds.

If I Call Love, Who Will Answer?

Gargoyles and winged lions.
        Bridges and parks.
                The gold angel bearing aloft
a cross in the shadow of the winter palace.

A chained bear on its side in the square,
        around which a crowd has gathered.
                It has possibly been drugged.
Little children can come up

to pet its matted fur, feel its flanks
        rise and fall with ragged breath.
                Like everything torn out of place,
it reeks of the momentous.

But isn't that how it is under every façade?
        Especially where light looks the most
                severe, where the lines try their best
to hold in, deflect, contain.

Graeae

Every so often she's roused by a call
        from the other side of the world—

her possibly senile, possibly-afflicted-
        with-dementia mother has reduced

her sister to tears yet again.
        She's flown into another of her rages:

screaming in the driveway, disheveled
        idol from antiquity, house keys a-dangle

and lashed together by a rope of shoelaces
        around her waist. She shakes her fists

at invisible enemies she claims have stolen
        her money and jewels, the new cell phone

which she may have forgotten she gave
        to the ne'er-do-well nephew

who came with threats when she had
        no more cash to give. Once

she may have counted herself among
        the town's great ladies—presiding

at meetings and tea, going to movie
        premieres on the arm of her late

husband. The woman she was
        in that past is as alien to the one

who used to go to daily Mass and the one
        she is now: crone shuffling in and out

of drafty rooms, banging doors at midnight,
       cursing those she lives with—

They tiptoe around, trying to do her bidding;
       failing, always failing. When company calls

she's demure and long-suffering. What
       she says, what she thinks, what she wants:

three separate destinies housed in the same
       body, furious at the same callous life—

passing the same eye and tooth
       from one gnarled hand to the other.

I Don't Have Feelings for the Angel

I've heard of *The Angel of History*;
read about it in works of both
poetry and philosophy, accounts
of wars after which, naturally, the dead

wind up entombed or buried in the soil,
their gravestones adorned with carved
cherubs, soot-stained angels with somber
faces—Their heavy wings plume

downward, as if never to fly again. The Angel
holds its hands aloft: as if to anoint, as if
to gesture at the immensity and utter
inaddressability of everything that's

taken place, that's been done to you—
which is why it's often easier to still
the lips into silence, easier to stand
through the years as if made of stone,

as if stone doesn't fracture.
Has the Angel seen everything I've
always wanted to know, that no one
will tell me? Has it witnessed how

and where two bodies made the seed
sown into the soil of my becoming? In every
photograph I have, my father's brow is mine;
but I can't figure which parts of Mother's

younger sister's face to claim: whether he took
it in his hands, if he was gentle, if he was rough,
if he demanded some show of loyalty that couldn't
answer except in surrender, in the belief

there was no other choice. No one ever talks
about such things, and so the details are
lost; but since history is even then what
has happened, can the Angel therefore be held

complicit? Is the Angel the sponsor who
looked on without stopping any of what it saw:
in a back room, in a bathroom stall, in the kitchen
when no one else was at home? I don't have feelings

for the Angel. I do have feelings for the people
it turned into my kin; for the bonds it multiplied
in ways they also strained to wear through the years
they lived together: fiercely guarding secrets,

loving and hating and fighting in the same space.
In the end, they are who they are—their portraits
thumbnailed into every side story, their skin oils
part of every bit of furniture in which they rested

their bodies; their blurred reflections haunting me
from the bottom of every pot into which I'll ever
cast my gaze. *Love and Duty, Love and Hate, Honor,
History*: I want to say *Enough,* but the Angel isn't done

with whatever it thinks it wants to do. I want to say
*Tell me everything exactly as it happened, tell me what
it means* though I know there are secrets they've taken
to the grave that even the Angel could never know.

II

Sparrow Palace

I return to that chipped edifice shaped
        like a cake topper, its tiny doors leading
to drafty corridors and abandoned rooms,
        elaborate latticework a gnawed confection

crumbling in the sun. In that moldy tower, what
        did I think I was if not a kind of prisoner
of love? I wove my miniature shrouds and practiced
        tapping Morse code on the walls until

Father caught me, or finally I tired of walking
        labyrinths into the floorboards. Night
after night, from one of the rooms, I heard Mother
        sing "Last Song" without irony, cupping

her hands to her breast. She kept singing
        even when I refused to accompany her.
In summer, she divided seeds from yellow
        pods in the green jackfruit's hollow.

But its flesh was forbidden, for fear my body
        would send ripe streamers of scent
too early into the world. Instead, I sat
        popping stale bits of roasted corn

into my mouth, occasionally tossing some
        to pigeons in the courtyard. In those days
the doors of my chest had not yet swung open;
        my cheeks had not been daubed

with a paste of water and my own first blood.
        There wasn't yet a parapet on whose edge
a flickering thought could sharpen into hunger
        with a body, with a pair of wings.

Elegy for Loss

When the cleaning women come again it takes much more
cajoling before you let them into your house, let them

scrub the grime caked over nearly a year on floorboards,
bathroom tile, kitchen cabinets, shelves still groaning

with the weight of every last rusted spoon and knick-knack
you salvaged from your other life—Then, you were known

as wife of the retired judge everyone remembers, dapper
to your own handcrafted elegance. Perlita says, gently,

Let us wipe the dust off this picture frame, then
you can put it back in your bedroom. Nothing is

going to disappear. How long has it been since you lifted
the faded mustard flannel draped over the Winkelmann

upright piano, since anyone ran fingers over its
yellowed keys? Trembling mallets wrapped in wool

stop just short of the soundboard. Has the refrigerator
light gone out, or has someone disconnected the appliance?

Extravagance, surplus poured around the ordinary:
for you, slipping a half stick of butter into a pot

of pasta; or saying that in some countries, men show admiration
for women by slapping their butts. Do you remember going

into the shoe store downtown at least once a month? Now
I'm told you shuffle around in a pair of plastic hospital

slippers from your recent confinement. The last time we speak
on the telephone, you cycle from crying over your empty bank

accounts to railing about the loss of your house. How
to write about a room with a bare light bulb, a threadbare

sofa, half a moon broken clean in the sky from its shadow?
This elegy for everything we've lost, and lost between us.

On Keeping

She spoke the languages of flour,
of salt, of pepper. From her hands

issued heat and steam;
from her hips, small

constellations still learning
the lessons of combustion.

Once, we tore newspapers
into tiny squares and fed them

to the maw of a makeshift stove.
Windows lit up with low-

wattage light. It was enough
to see by—enough to weigh

into logs and stud with dried
fruit, cloves, honey: they kept

nearly six months in tins,
tightly wrapped, unopened.

When she flew away, a moth
circled the milky light.

The kitchen drawers exhaled
all spice from their hearts.

Decryption

All these years and still you
    couldn't make me. Can't make me call this man *Uncle.*
Ever since he touched me—Here, there, here.
    Girl in short bangs, inverted bowl of hair.
I no longer sucked my thumb but I was very young.
    Knife in the maw of a pain dumb now but still blunt.
Moods come over me. I think them unrelated, until
    outrage raps on the door. No one knew what to make of it.
Quit before the toxic kingdom settles, I tell myself.
    Supper molders on the table while I compose documents
under internal dictation. Why not now, rather than never?
    Why rewind the spool to that part where it snags?
You've yanked it back; and each time string a new-old bead:
    Zamaro, zambombo, grosero. Sinvergüenza. Antipático.
X-Acto knife blades layer silhouettes. Edge to edge,
    vivid outlines thicken the image, buff dry some of the fury.
Thanks to our theory of production, some 18,000+ days have now
    rolled off the factory machine since that unwelcome insinuation—
Please note: this is not proof that nothing ever happened.
    Neon is to vacation as medieval tapestry is to confession.
Locate the lion, the unicorn; the bird, the cage, the ferret.
    Justice is a shorthand that takes the longest, longest time.
Heresy has the same number of syllables as honesty.
    For my sake, I walk through every room at night, testing
doorknobs, light switches, typewriter keys. No apology has come.
    By what right should bitter roots be made to compost in honey?

Smoke

Do you want to visit
your father? she said.
          And we did. He was wan

but jovial in the bed cranked
up to receiving position;
          his friends played cards

on the cotton sheet and reached
for shot glasses on the side table.
          This was back in the day

when no one said *No Smoking*
or *You can't bring such things*
          in here. The balcony doors

overlooked the parking lot,
where you'd think the air was still
          pristine despite the spew

of diesel from trucks and jeeps.
You'd think it was some cheap
          hotel, checkerboard tile

floors, something like the set
of *Casablanca*; or grainy around
          the edges in that Polaroid way

as Mrs. Robinson turns to Benjamin
in *The Graduate*, still holding
          aloft her cigarette. I wonder what

the good sisters at Notre Dame
de Lourdes Hospital would say
          if they knew he'd taken me

to see those films? In 1968,
I was seven. *Close your eyes,*
           he ordered, just before

the salacious scenes.
Obedience, curiosity's boring
           older sibling. I can almost hear

his defense: no one ever died
from learning how to live
           in the world. The good

sisters made clucking noises
but also brought in ashtrays.
           His friends tore off

the silver tab on a box
of Salem Menthol Lights
           and tapped smartly on one end.

No, no, he smiled
and shook his head. *This is it,*
           he declared. *I'm quitting.*

Where the Seed Scattered

She took us through dense rows out back
where fennel spurted lavish through the ground—

branched green tendrils now hardening to husks
amid long growth of asparagus. Inside round

shells no bigger than my thumb, next season's
growth waited to root in layers above the clay.

Beneath the pear trees, in the grass, wasps
buzzed in drunken stupor: the body in decay

still giving of its sugar, its thick and milky sap,
before composting into soil. Nearby, the flames

of peppers gashed the undersides of leaves: trapped
heat of bird chilies, the smoky mildness of shishitos.

She said it was the only way she'd ever planted:
allowing what fell, to fall where it would.

Dream of Flight, with Bus Attendant

Like all the other girls at the ticket counter,
this one's young, smartly dressed in red and yellow.

Her jaunty cap, aslant, dips slightly below
the brow. You wonder if she'd be better

off walking an aircraft's narrow aisles,
pushing carts of water, soda, coffee, tea,

foil-wrapped peanuts, crackers, cheese—
than listing left and right as the express

bus lumbers down the mountain road. It's raining hard
and the cracked window gaskets leak, so she stoops

every few rows to apply a layer of old newspapers
under our feet. She comes back shortly, still

smiling: old-fashioned one-hole ticket punch
in hand, settling us in for the six-hour ride.

Synecdoche

(Magellan's Cross and Basilica del Santo Niño, Cebu)

A part for the whole, the whole for the part:
    one reason we collect souvenirs, make gifts,
bring proof of states we've passed through

and survived. The reason we wrap and tuck
    in tissue, fold away in plastic or in chests
with cedar chips before it's even clear

why, or what it is we're saving—That day,
    for instance, lining up with other pilgrims
at the shrine, a hot wind blowing through

the cupola from the sea; and the native women
    clad in broadcloth skirts of brown and yellow
swayed their hips in the Sinulog, chanting

prayers into which they'd braided our names—
    safe travels, good health, love, luck, wealth:
the usual pleas the faithful might bring

before any deity. A couple of fifty-
    peso bills, and they pressed into our hands
a clutch of candles: blue, green, yellow,

some of which we could light and fix
    atop the marble base beneath Magellan's Cross,
the rest to take with us on our return. A plaque

affixed there told of how this tindalo wood
    that people stroked with reverent fingers
was not the cross itself the explorer planted

on the beach in 1521, perhaps more grateful
     for the end of that wretched sea voyage
than for the complex details of conquest

to follow—but that he did not actually
     live to see unfold. The artifact itself lay
inside the wood as a violin might nestle

darkly in its case, preventing the overzealous
     from chipping off pieces, splintery tickets
to the miraculous. A courtyard away

inside the Basilica, longer lines snaked through
     stone-paved hallways for the chance to look
into the glass case holding the image

of the child Jesus: robes of blood-red velvet
     embellished with gold, Magellan's gift
to Rajah Humabon's wife after the pair

were baptized and made to pledge allegiance
     to the Spanish crown. Four decades and another
expedition later, Miguel López de Legazpi torched

the villages where he claimed the natives
     had grown hostile; a soldier found
the image intact in a charred wooden box,

though fisherfolk were in the habit
     of telling other stories—the kinds in which
holy statues abandoned their altars at night

and traveled through the countryside,
     dipping bare feet and hems of garments
in the mud to come to the aid of the poor

and ailing. How could transcendence
    newly spring in a stricken world where
mystery is traded for chance, politicians'

promises, cheap knockoffs? Awaiting
    our turn, it was unnerving to see
so many devotees rap violently

with their hands, with their knuckles
    on the glass that kept the idol
in its separate, airless space.

Some sobbed, some wept quietly;
    all of them cried *Pit Senyor! Pit Senyor!*
before dropping a coin into the box.

Pit Senyor ~ An abbreviated form of the Cebuano expression "sangpit sa Señor,"
meaning to supplicate the Señor Santo Niño or Holy Child Jesus, one of the
Roman Catholic titles of the Child Jesus associated with his religious image
venerated as miraculous by Filipino Catholics.

Prodigal

Risk is but the fact you have to go
        too far. And if that's so, is it still risk

after you've returned? Peering through rain-
        slashed windows of the bus that twisted,

ponderous lozenge, through a narrow gorge,
        I hardly recognized the city, every hillside

shingled with dark roofs, every road choked
        with vehicles in which disconsolate motorists

sat waiting to arrive at their destinations.
        When we alighted at the station, it was evening

and the sidewalks swarmed with schoolchildren
        walking home under shared umbrellas, men

and women in the taxi queue. The noodle shops
        and cafés were packed: everyone at their tables

bent over notebooks, waiting for some small
        bright pleasure to arrive in the form of food

and drink. Every now and then, groups pressed together
        and smiled on cue—girls with smooth, fair faces,

eyes beguiling as butterflies with that upward sweep
        of eyeliner at the corners; boys turning up two fingers

to make the peace sign close to their cheeks—
        as someone held at arm's length a cellphone

with the camera setting turned to auto selfie.
        As soon as the aperture shut, it opened again.

And I had returned, it was true, and stood
　　　　　but a moment in the vestibule before my own

connections came to claim me. In the days following,
　　　　　friend after friend exclaimed, *O but the years*

haven't changed you at all. Among my kin,
　　　　　shyly, we broke the intervening years into pieces

to dip in soup or coffee so they could soften. Both
　　　　　times, the buoyant and the poignant, I could hardly

contain, could hardly tell apart. Until I left anew,
　　　　　I did not know what depth of sadness possessed me:

the waters of that river never stayed still,
　　　　　as Heraclitus warned long before. How they

would wash my feet, but never the same way twice.

Portraits

Your father never so much as washed a plate
in his whole life, my mother once said to me.
I have to concede this is true, thinking back

on our lives in the old green bungalow that used to be
one of the president's summer houses—I forget which.
The story was that when we arrived to take

possession, his portrait (not father's but
the president's) hung in a grimy hallway until
it was taken down and everything could be mopped

and dusted, things set in place. I don't know
where the painting went; I never saw it again.
In fact I can't remember any of its

details. As for my father, though he was
fastidious about his appearance, he never sat
for any formal portrait. In high school, for an art

project I tried to capture their likenesses on canvas,
working from a photograph—my smiling mother
on the left, wearing coral lipstick

and her best pearls; my father on the right,
in a suit with a fine houndstooth check. I worked
to find some faithfulness to the picture,

and must have succeeded: he said he did not like
the way the corners of his mouth were set, as if
to make him look so unforgiving; nor the too-

somber cast of his brow. The oils still pliable,
I did my best to lift and soften. I knew, after all,
from watching: how much it cost to inhabit the face

he mustered daily for that world of encounter
with others we barely knew—The men in silk ties
wrapped in a haze of cigarette smoke, their women

a frothy coterie. It was a time when we
were supposed to know our place in the world,
learn the kinds of work we were allowed to do.

First Night: In Mother's House

Stay, she says, plumping up pillows
on a makeshift bed. The window frames
are painted red, the rough floor

thin with yawning gaps
through which I can hear
the wind razor through

crowded houses on the hill.
The rain is overgenerous
and doesn't stop. I count

the frames she's nailed up, willy-
nilly, on the wall—Pictures
I painted when I was a girl:

rivers and expansive fields,
still lifes, canvases suffused
with roses, bright lemons fallen

from a faceted crystal bowl:
metaphor too for the old
life we used to have. And though

I could have, I did not visit
the street where, a lifetime ago,
we'd made our home—

I feared I couldn't bear the sight
of ruin; or worse, of empty space.
Days later, when we rode past,

I was grateful for the new
gas station and the downpour,
relentless, that obscured the view.

Volta

I'm told I was a homely child—unlovely
stripling with scabbed legs, crooked teeth—

given to various ailments: asthmatic wheeze,
one gash above my lip that marred my smile;

blistering hives, a wart they tried to file
off my finger and excise with a squeeze

of muriatic acid. And though my knees
felt lunar, my budding mind found fertile

rooms with other kinds of mirrors: quickly,
I learned to lose myself in books, whole

worlds beneath awareness, where no one
told me I would never this or that—Pity

a kind of bread to change the smallest bird:
plumped up by rain, dry crumb no longer dun.

Gathering Figs in the Rain

In the rain, globe after globe
of shimmering purple; high up,
      tenanted in broad scalloped robes—

No rungs for the feet, no stirrups;
thus always the one the heart really wants
      is just out of reach. Jewel on a dark stub,

ticket to certain sweetness: no other response
seems fitting except to peel you off the branch,
      fingertips glossed with drops of sap. Chance

turned into choice: green that held out until blanched
in high summer heat, then cooled as clouds rolled in,
      pregnant, unable to stay in their own skin. Stanch

the wound that bleeds by pressing down and touching—
Teardrop shape, honeyed light bulb. What you chose and what
      dropped into your hand. Stand still. The rain is thinning.

Open House

~ Bahay na bato: middle class, colonial Filipino house, circa 1850

A harp in the center of the living room,
meant to reflect the shimmer of wind.

*

Seamed overlap of curved shells
that skirt the length of walls.

*

Under every cane-striped lounging chair,
a sepia-stained chamber pot.

*

Fleur-de-lis, geometry of sunken shapes: fine
debris of sweets and dust in ancient cookie stamps.

*

Lace the color of old tea. Swirled wood
that holds the secrets of four-posters.

*

Slippers of brocade, rows of glass
atomizers on the nightstand.

*

In the cool, high-ceilinged toilet, a two-
seater commode gives proof of their intimacy.

*

Beneath the balcony, frogs lisp on the cistern's
mossy lip: water source, hiding place; route to escape.

In the hotel with thin walls and the name of a poet,

you hear the busboys hail each other
on the sidewalk after midnight. You hear
a man expectorating in the bathroom of room 101—
the sound he makes, like someone drowning on dry land.
If it's true there are ghosts, you want to wait
for the one of your grandfather to materialize
and lead you by the hand down the grand staircase,
past tables laid with silver and candelabra
to the kitchen where he cleanly severed
the joints of fowl before he cooked them
in broth with ginger and squash. If it's true
that the rain will never cease, then the trail
of ants will lead from the hibiscus in the yard
to the bowl of honey in the larder; and you'll eat
spoonful after spoonful so as to never fear
the mold so freely papering the ceilings,
to keep it from ever taking root in your lungs.
If it's true—that dream you used to have of hovering
over a billowed sheet in the shape of a sea: then
the green and white days in its aftermath
are only a pause, a door in the garden
through which women in evening dresses
have gone in search of the transcendental;
into which the long afternoon siestas
of childhood have all but disappeared.

She Remembers Her Father's Blue Eyes

In a country of dark-eyed men
his eyes were anomaly—

Cloudy blue like stones dredged
from the river's shallow depths,

myth of a town somewhere in Spain
that gave him his middle name.

He was stern as a citadel
or a fortress on a hill,

then disarming as the old-
world charm of a soft wax seal.

Childless forty years before she
came along, broken open he curated

every simple line drawing,
doted on her childish scrawl.

Her declamations and arpeggios
were dedicated to him, paragon

of perfection, industrious at
virtue. Even now, at the whiff

of Old Spice or English Leather,
she straightens her spine, checks

the angle of the ruler; lays
the curve of letters on paper

before carefully blotting
the fountain pen's tip.

Caravan

Fregata Magnificens

Absolution: that faint smudge, landing spot, port
             where the compass points north.

Buy your tickets, or call
             the hawkers. Not cheap for

chance passengers, considering
             the nature of accommodations.

Don't you always get the joke
             when the joke's on you?

Economics simply means there are
             more people than there are seats.

First class these days gets you a pack
             of peanuts, maybe. Frigate birds

get more lift just from cloud hopping.
             Among the unwaterproofed horde,

how many have papers, how many
             are undocumented? And yet they log

incomparable mileage. Their other skill:
             purloining what's heaved over as

jetsam. In other words,
             working it so other birds throw up

krill and squid, flying fish,
             plankton. We should be so

lucky. To be continuously aloft,
>	with only the briefest inter-

missions for food—After so long
>	a journey, who even recalls what

need or nightmare first
>	catapulted us here?

O to soar and soar, to enter through
>	warm white hems of cloud, have air fill

pneumatic bones, lighter than girdles
>	fused to the shoulder joint.

Quicksilver gloss on the belly;
>	everything else dark, mottled,

rustic as cyanotype. What bright gashes
>	of color! We're prized for such things, made

spectacular as bodies in a fair.
>	What do you have there in that

throat pouch shaded deep scarlet? Do you
>	have for me letters, loves, poems?

Uncountable miles have come between
>	me and the future, me and the past.

Veering ever onward, I try to shut
>	my ears to the tumult et cetera.

Will you glide a little way with me, ransack the dips
>	for freshwater? If these jaunts were through

xysts lined with trees—something
                fragrant like linden, like fireflower—perhaps

yaw velocity might compute differently. Perhaps
                the wandering body that's forgotten what it's like at

zero motion might sight at last a distant ring
                of islands, a cliff of chalky white in the final mile.

System

The hornet mines
pulp for her paper house.

My house is fragile too:
a wave could knock it flat,

a deadly gust of wind.
Cold coil of winter,

unholy fire of summer.
If only I could gird

the windows with a low,
unceasing drone, fasten

stings with locks
on all the gates.

Texture of the Lost

What poverty is amplified by stacks of moving boxes? Somewhere in the depths of one: a pile of unpaired socks, a spoon without its fork, a book whose frontispiece is missing. In the grooves of the madeleine pan, a memory that sticks and will never come off. Are the simplest things the best? In her mind, she subtracts one piece of furniture after another. He has a turkey sandwich on wheat every single day. She can't. She needs to mix things up, so her taste buds remember the yellow of pineapples, the bright bitter green of kale. Where posters were once held to the wall with little bits of putty, now there are oil spots darker than paint. Once, as she stood in front of a shop window, the blur of a passing truck wrote letters in reverse on her forehead.

Half-Life

"to tell someone that you lived,
and this is how it was." ~ Sean Thomas Dougherty

If I count the time I've spent
living in this body minus the years
spent trying to summon the fragments
it left behind, I wind up with string
the color of smoke, a plume dark
as a dream of birds rowing the air,
silvering the night with their cries—
What kind of promise is it to say
everything's made beautiful and sleek
by effort, though it never arrives?
My desire is also perpetually disheveled
by desire. Yet if I count the morsels
of bread and meat that touched my tongue,
they would only be proof of my shame—
Who can tell what the gods throw
in the water for sport, and how to fashion
a net to bring it back? How could I thrive
in this body while my other body, my heart,
rocked itself to sleep in a silent house?

Buttonholes

Back then I had no words
for hands that emerged from
the pressed darkness of a crowded
movie theatre—all of us behind
the balcony rail, standing room only,
slapstick on the screen as the hero
clutched his boxer shorts and hopped
from the heat of the hornet's nest
bulging on his behind. How did my
blouse buttons become undone?
Instinctively my elbows became
shards, became flailing
as the roars and laughter
rose in waves in the theatre.
I can write this now with no
guttering sound from my throat,
no constriction in my airways,
though sometimes the simplest
gesture I make still undresses me.

Letter to —— in Increments

Dear ——, I haven't written in years. What made me think of it today, of you? When we came home this evening, small bodies of gnats and moths were outlined against the door. We fumbled for the keys, and in that small beat of time I felt almost embarrassed to see how many had battered themselves against that rectangle of shimmering white. In the garden, the ferns push up, insistent through a skin of plastic and a thin layer of mulch. The August sky is waning. Another year is almost gone.

Dear ——, I started this letter last night in hopes that I would finish it. I looked for a stamp and wanted to use my good pen; I filled it with ink the color of burnt wheat from a bottle on the shelf. There was a young woman in my classroom whose right thigh was bandaged. She had no crutches, but walked with a limp. She was in a motorcycle accident yesterday. A driver speeding up to merge didn't see her, not even her hair dyed feverish green. Her anger and self-pity still crackled freshly like a halo around her. She pulled a chair from the next row and put up her leg.

Dear ——, when you were my age did you worry about dying? Did you worry about leaving anyone behind? When she called last week, my daughter told me that in her college there is a new one-credit class called "Adulting." They teach students things about "real life" like how to do their laundry (separate the whites), fill out checks for deposit, how frequently they should change their sheets, how to tell when the milk has gone bad. She couldn't believe it, she said. Sheets. Milk. Laundry.

Dear ——, do you know how table legs jut out and bump against your knees depending on how the chairs are positioned around it? I tried to change the way the seats were arranged, tried to move them like a compass or a clock hand pushed very slightly out of orbit. In less than two days they were back again where they used to be. I know someone who was given a different office space; she moved everything and laid the objects out exactly the way they were, on her new desk. Do you remember the little purse you gave me when I was a child? The one shaped like a girl's face under the broad brim of a straw hat? When we were out and I was bored, I'd suck on the little cluster of green rubber grapes adorning the ribbon. I still remember the way they tasted, the way something needless claims obsessive attention.

When I Think I Could Be Beautiful

Though I too live in a blur of worlds, I am one
shade of brown: my blood not as obviously mixed.

Who gave me this nose? I have no dimples. I have a brow
broad as a page. The eyes tell when I am smiling.

And eyebrows constitute a language of their own. Never
asleep, they are two republics separated by a bridge.

Do you know the power of discarded fish bones?
I know delight can interchange with dilate.

I've strung the dried stumps of my daughters' birth
cords on a safety pin; this is one way I keep them close.

Do you know the sound the tin bucket makes, the shape
of its mouth as it looks at the sky from inside the well?

In the birdhouse made from hollowed-out wood: wasps
coming and going. They are not angry yet, only nesting.

The ginger flower's torch burns with scent in the middle
of the garden. Not even the rain can put it out.

Sensorium

She tells me
about the hive of bees in her ears:

their dialect of drone and fuzz
drowns out everyday sounds—

water from the tap
overflowing the bathroom pail,

kettle straddling the blue
stove flame on its highest setting.

I knock and knock on the metal gate,
hoping the radio network

of nerves translates the signals.
She tells me she's sold

or pawned off most of her jewelry.
But she puts in my hands a box;

in its tissue folds twin
silver peacocks dangle

from French hoops: their tail
feathers wired, trembling.

III

North

This is where I learn to be
completely alone, even among others.

Frost but never snow, late in December
or at the beginning of the year.

Beautiful crust of ice rimming every head
of cabbage, so the farmers wring their hands.

Think of the cold and its serrated edge,
the frozen pellets dropped by goats.

Eidetic memory: black cutouts of trees
against a brilliant sky.

How wine made from fermented rice
is sweet for a moment in the mouth

before a cloud of fire descends
into the empty gut.

Looking for Lorenzo

Visiting my hometown for three weeks in summer, I stayed
with my youngest daughter in a hotel whose name made me think
of a famous poet from Santiago de Chuco. Built in 1909, so
        much of the architecture was still the same—

slate-colored shingles angled as if on purpose against weeks
of pouring rain; dark wooden interiors, thin, uninsulated walls
that barely kept out the cold. I asked for an extra blanket
        at the front desk. The girl on duty said shyly, *Extra*

30, Ma'am. I asked *Dollars? per day?* At which
she shook her head— *No, pesos; 30 only one time, Ma'am;*
then later, knocked softly to bring a thin blanket that felt
        like military wool. I thought of my grandfather Lorenzo—

he came to work here as a cook when he was only 19,
and stayed five years. This was during Peacetime, before WWII.
I don't know how old Lorenzo was when my mother was born
        in the city, but I know they lived for a time

in Jungletown, parts of which I glimpsed from the windows
of the hotel dining room. Each morning, we made our way
to breakfast down the graceful curving staircase.
        The wait staff quietly went about their business—

buffing the floors, pouring coffee, bringing trays
of bread or mountain rice, platters of eggs and venison,
local sausages, relish, dried fish. I sent back the sugar
        and milk. I asked for bottled water; I asked

for local honey, for finger bowls of onions and fresh
tomatoes, for cup after cup of brewed Benguet coffee—
just to extend the time for small
        conversation. One of our regulars, so boyish

in face and slight in the loose gray colonial
porter-styled uniform, told us the day before we left
that his name was Choco; he wouldn't see us again,
         because his baby was sick and he was taking

the next day off. You have a baby? I'd never have guessed,
I said. He said he was a communication arts graduate
but could not yet find a better job; had a wife
         and child to support. I settled the bill and left

what I hoped was a generous tip. The rain never
once let up during our visit. I never saw
the ghost of Lorenzo in the musty hallways, never saw
         hint of the one white suit he wore, his signature.

Dead Woman's Float

Clasp your knees to your chest. Pretend
you're an egg in the water; slowly peel
each limb away from the body. Relax.
Let the choppy waves wash over you,
the agitations caused by your starfish
children. This isn't the first time you've
had to take the extra beating that's
really meant for the absent parent.
Resist the urge to try a Muay Thai
move with fists, elbows, knees, shins.
Observe the sandy bottom, the graceful
lines of kelp; the blue-green bubbles,
prismatic, floating to the surface:
the real masters in the art of holding
the breath. When the sun's thermometer
eventually cools, stand up slowly.
Let the water stream gently down
your hair. No matter how many times
they've seen this, they'll swear you
are a monster rising from the depths.
All the more reason to steer clear
of clamshells, leave the foam alone.

Orchard

It's fall, season of the apple—iconic
fruit of this America, mounds of excess
littering the grounds of orchards
from want of migrant hands to pick
the harvest clean: their red the banner
of every girl or woman who tips her head up
to the knowledge of her power—which means
she can see the way things work in the world,
and chooses not to be shamed any longer
for calling it. For what did the hissing
in the leaves tell her that she didn't
already know, or the laughter behind
closed doors when she ran, groping
her way out? *Don't pretend you don't
know what I want,* said every snake
in the grass. Survival means no one
dies, but someone is forced to take
the fall: the smallest bird, the lowest
fruit—though the fruit isn't to blame
for its sheen, nor the star for marking
the place where its light was last seen.

Madrigal

Of course there's a singing bone,
a treasure, a magic that's been stolen.

There's a king fallen into a stupor, a kingdom
of fields littered with empty cerveza bottles.

He roams the hallways whose walls bear
the imprint of his fists, unable to recognize

any of his daughters. Of course one of them
is determined to get things right again,

says she would do anything.
What will it take to bring him back?

Perhaps there is virtue if not blessedness
in oblivion. Perhaps it's simply more difficult

to tell which rhetoric is vacant—the low-
frequency hum of a radio station that's always

been too far out of range; or the crickets
whose voices come back, night after night.

Underststudy

At the army hospital, whose nipple
did they put in my mouth after I
slid out and through her? That first
night and the rest that came after,

whose arms received the wrapped
bundle of me in those days before
Pampers or vinyl diaper covers,
that soon I must have soaked

with my own effluvia? I know
they never were farther apart
or closer than that day; later,
through the winding years, one

was always in the next room,
or a floor below in the split-
level bungalow we shared.
To this day,

what they knew suspends
like a gauzy drape above my head,
around my shoulders as I sift
in my own rooms, trying to write

again toward their secrets: older
and younger, sisters yoked by that
most domestic space of the womb
and what issues from it.

In what way and what did it signify
how each in turn or at the same time
was loved by my father? For he
is the other shadow in this

unfinished tale. Two being dead,
only one of them perhaps could put
my questions to rest—but she sits
in the house of her diminishing

faculties, unconscious
of the echolalia that's crept
into her speech. Though I'll put
these threads aside as the hour

grows late, never do they
leave me completely alone—
at table, at the stove, attending
to my work or my own

housekeeping, I'll feel the fierce
press of their shadows in the old
ways: triumvirate to all I do,
waking, sleeping, dreaming.

Sketches in a Genealogy

1

To everyone, she was Little
Mother, mother's younger sister;

sometime shelter, confidant, friend—
The maids in neighbors' houses, especially,

came to seek her advice:
deboning fish, preserving fruit,

extracting savor from crushed heads
of shrimp. To all, she gave unstinting

service in her prime: from dawn to dusk,
the only acolyte at kitchen sink and stove;

red-knuckled hand that scrubbed soiled linens,
that cut our morning bread. I never knew

her secrets or her true desires.
Though clearly, having had me young

then given me up years before she had
three others, her heart could not

have been immune. One afternoon, while
in her care after school in kindergarten,

she put away the laundry and took my hand,
saying we would walk to the plaza and have

lunch at a Chinese restaurant. She put
her finger on my lips, and her lips said

Don't tell. The rest is a blur
of noise and oily smells. And then I was

too involved with strands of slippery
noodles in my bowl to notice anything else

about the man who sat next to her at our table,
only that she could not keep her eyes from his.

2

A loop of metal
& a clasp at the end
of a chain

Two french wires
& the bones
of miniature chandeliers

Four prongs that seat
a gem of doubtful
pedigree

This window light
is mute to tell
what they cost

but they're given
now to me—The only
instruction that I

remember who I am
& that a stone has facets
time whittles constantly

3

Rain again, with nothing much to do but stay
in place. Looking through moldy albums, I pry
the plastic sheets from still slightly gummy
backing in search of something I might want

to take away with me. I find the one
where we've brought the children—the two
older girls under the age of eight, the newborn
on my lap—to the park in what used to be

the American base. It was December
so I'd wrapped a shawl around my shoulders,
one end conveniently shielding the baby
as I nursed her in the car. We'd fought

again, about what I won't or can't remember
anymore, not even fitfully. He may have slammed
the car door, leading the two toward the playground.
I'm sure the children noticed, but in the way

that children do when they're that age, the swings
and slides and roundabouts claimed their full attention.
And the flinty sunlight that chipped continuously
at the trees poured quivering tumblers full

on me too where I sat—One child
at my breast asleep, her sisters bending and spooling
through painted hoops, all unaware of how distant
I felt from joy or certainty of place—

How long did I sit like that, tears
coursing down my face? A uniformed guard bent
toward my window when she passed, and asked
if everything was alright: her eyes meeting mine

implied that I might trust her if
I needed to. I know I shook my head.
I might have refused to look at her again
for fear that I might truly come undone.

Material

It's telling, the things
we return to: what's in those parts
where the looping frame hiccups to a stop,
shudders, tries again only to gain vertigo,

not momentum. For instance, those figures
in the shadow play that chased each other around
the garden or breakfast table, making javelins
of the heavy silverware, shattering a glass

butter dish, then crumpling to the floor
in a torrent of tears. The man slams a door
on the way out, declaring he never wants
to come back; and the woman with the shape

of a growing moon pressed into her body
goes from house to house, pleading, knocking.
Or the way the light looked that evening,
temperatures plummeting but no snowfall yet

when medical transport came to take
the girl, and all there was for several
days was the silence of not knowing—
This is the thick sludge, the slurry

to work through year after year. Holidays
bring them into uncomfortable focus, or provide
the opportunity to turn them into a raging
bonfire. In either case, the threads make

a patterned braid, the lines draw such
a familiar circle in the dirt. And you must
step in, bow formally to the shape that crouches
in wait, and which you always wind up wrestling.

Ghost Crab

~ Ocypode quadrata

Salt freckling the air, signature
of the decomposing under every

chassis that wheels across the sand.
It doesn't care if the light is translucent

on skin, it doesn't want to hear
the constant echo of *I, I, I*

on every wind stream. Past the strandline,
litter swept in by a recent storm, among which

scavenger birds conduct sweeping investigations.
Blue flesh, ammonite of lyrical spirals—

I can't help it if I sway, dizzy
in the labyrinth. Every hull I pick up

on the beach is clear warning,
though when I tilt my head the sky

still froths with what refuses
to be deleted. So many forms

from which to choose: fine fuzz, pale
thread, needle spinning on the surface.

Cracked carapace, heft of a bone left to dry; ashes
like bits of language, left in the pan after the fire.

How to Enter the Dark

When it is too quiet at night
    I wonder what is troubling the waters;

whether the banked clouds we saw
    at sundown, their colors rich but muted

like a medieval tapestry, are merely
    a screen that hasn't risen yet

on the next act. Will there be
    columns of smoke, towns going

under water, colonies of dead
    bees scattered like gold beads

on the grass? When they announce
    the evacuation order, you look

around and can't decide which
    of the things that could fit

into one backpack could answer to
    the description of essential.

Weren't you taught all, all
    is important to the living body,

everything that could be grafted to it
    as well as shorn away? And everything

is also already in your heart—Memory
    of feasts made by hand that now

your same hand empties the icebox of,
    for fear of the power going out,

the meat and butter going bad, the wilt
    and ruin of even the thinnest stalk

of green. Regret: the wrapper around
    a gift that hasn't been torn open;

that hasn't opened in you some stay
    on time. And at night, it's all you can do

to not give in to the dark immediately.
    To count slowly even as you enter it.

Indenture

Isn't it always about our relationship to time:
how we bargain, attempt to wrestle with

the impossible, rewrite the memos that read
as intractable sentences? Those summer months

when the cruel grandmother had come to live
with us, past midnight I heard her cries

from the room down the hall: calling for her son,
for water, for the bedpan. And yet he never

was the one to attend to her afflictions,
but the daughter-in-law she treated

for decades as someone not good enough
for the favorite, her unico hijo. Though muffled,

the emanations of their pain were quilled
and tufted into every mattress. How pitifully

they shuffled in their robes and house slippers
around the breakfast table; how meanly laid

the lines around their eyes, when each
was barely looking. I thought I'd try to make

some things easier: fetch and carry, put away,
my small hands clasping the water pitcher.

One morning, rushing ahead of Grandmother,
thinking to open the heavy door before

she got there—how could I anticipate
she'd trip and fall? Though she recovered

from that accident, her later years
were split between wheelchair and bed.

Imperious until the end, she became the idol
whose whims we served: smoking her thin

cigars, rasping orders until her grip
on life at last unfixed. No one perceived

my small intention; no comfort knowing
bones are more brittle after a certain age.

Field Notes

What choice has the ox when it comes
to the edge of the field but turn

and walk to the other end? I am always
trying to balance the weight of the yoke,

the way it slides down shoulders
from the friction of years. Even when

it's put away, I have a manner
of walking that signals furrow

and stubble before I open my mouth.
If a dove touches down, if a phoenix

or a tongue of flame in the middle
of the field, I'd feed it whatever

it is I carry if I knew how. How to hear
the sound of a different color? The bright-

ness of copper or gold, the shimmer
in the pause of just standing still.

Orchard

Speak, don't speak, or keep
        your counsel to yourself—
                see how to dress

for a few more years
        your cache of aches
                in neutral wrappers.

But take care
        not to leach out all
                the feeling—The child

must find a way
        to herself among
                the fruit that's fallen

from the tree: say this
        or green or gold while
                cradling the bruised.

Hortus Conclusus

(Enclosed garden; after Clive Hicks-Jenkins's The Enclosure; *oil pastel on paper)*

> *"Thou art all fair, my love;*
> *there is no spot in thee."* ~ *Song of Songs*

Ours used to be the second house on the right
from the top of the street, after De Castro's Sand
& Gravel and truck yard. There was an enclosure:
high fence of gray cemented cinderblock, a metal gate
      painted green that shut with deadbolts from the inside,

two lamps we turned on at dusk and kept
ablaze throughout the night to discourage thieves—
In better days there used to be soft, even carpeting
of grass on either side; a few rose bushes, poinsettias,
      clumps of comfrey and yerba buena bordering the porch;

profusion of bougainvillea climbing up
the siding. There was no spring, no sealed-up
fountain, no emblematic cistern overgrown by moss:
only a rusted tank we waited twice or thrice a week
      to fill, when it was the neighborhood's turn for water

rationing. There was no tree that fruited of foreign
apple or of pear, encircled by wrought iron or bright
barbs of wire. No totem patrolled this garden,
invisible by day or sleekly silvered by night,
      nor came to lay its head upon my lap.

Thus we came and went, watchful and watched,
trying to read each other's gestures as if stitched
in code, upon a tapestry. I'd tested the locks,
grown restive, found that even when I stayed
      out later after school, I'd merely ring

the doorbell and they'd let me in—
even the man who'd brought me back and came
to staying on for supper. Mouths met after, in damp,
furtive groping—as moths aimed their felted bodies
        at porch lights and fell, stunned upon impact.

When the family came to formally ask for
my hand in marriage, I don't recall the words actually
mentioned. Father and mother seemed resigned, as if
the unmentionable must have been breached; and the only
        way to make it right was set a date, reserve the church,

begin to list the ones who'd come to sponsor and to witness.
If they had asked, I could've told them an animal still laid
its gleaming brow and spiral of questions on the fleece
bedspread; but in time, even a silver overlay thins,
        loosens from its bonds of underlying metal.

A Reparation

There were some things I often had no
words or explanations for till after the fact
of their experiencing. For instance,

learning forms of the passive-aggressive:
that kind of maneuvering which rendered me
at once cold and hot, which made me second-

guess if not outright believe I must
have been the one at fault, said or done
the wrong thing, not known enough

to hold my place or keep the peace—
which meant, not raised a voice to demur,
to contradict, to question whatever

verdict or decision. How else explain the cold
shoulder, the silent disregard of conciliatory
gestures? Reading a tract on transcendental

meditation, I came upon this principle:
*Do not oppose a great force; retreat
until it weakens, then advance*

with resolution—something I took
as reassurance about the natural wisdom
of things; how, given time, their

logic would surface to defeat
all counterfeit versions of the truth.
And so it was, if nothing else, stunning

to find that he interpreted the same
in terms of a kind of extremism: he
was the great force never to be

opposed, especially when he'd flown
into one of his rages. Among the choice
parables held up during such times:

how he did not like the way
a former girlfriend dressed (too
provocative for his taste) and so

he followed her to the pool hall where
she'd gone to play a round with friends;
and without preamble, stripped her

of her V-neck blouse, neck to waist.
Even now I feel the slap of more than cold air.
I'm surprised I can bring myself to write

of this for the first time, in retrospect—
Perhaps it is the intervening years,
the gifts of age and distance, the need

to give at last an audience to all the sad
wraiths that lay and festered, airless and
unloved, in the dank basement of the mind.

Self-Portrait, Reconstructed with Heirloom Beads

Cold in the threaded mist of early morning,
in the mountains more than thirty years ago: a trip
made with a former lover ostensibly to photograph

the locals so I could render them afterwards
in pencil portrait sketches. We rented a room
with an adjacent toilet and bath: tall

metal drum of water; a ladle and small plastic pail.
Of course the underlying presumption had everything to do
with sex, so he was irritated when the first night

did not yield what he'd expected. Downstairs, in the morning,
waiting to walk down the path to a local cafeteria, I held
myself very still then slowly stretched an arm out, clump

of torn daffodils in my fingers offered to deer that had come
in the night to forage in the yard beside the inn. They moved
closer, the doe more skittish than her fawn—

their fear eventually overcome by some measure
of adaptation to jean-clad tourists there in droves
to hike the trails and visit citrus groves, climb

hand over hand down ropes to peer into the water-slicked
innards of underground caves. And I was so young then,
not yet familiar with the currents of my own desires—

Rough, untested edges of a self that knew only
it wanted to live somewhere else yet tried to hide
how terrified it was of its own clumsiness

and worldly ignorance. After breakfast,
when the proprietor asked if we'd like to see
her hidden trove of heirloom beads,

we followed her upstairs to her living
quarters, where she lifted from a chest
padlocked jewel cases and shook

strand after strand of strung carnelians,
smoky agates, beads cloud-milky, yellow
as the yolks of eggs or black-striped reds

that smelled as dusky as the earth. Handed down
from ancestors, they held the worth of cattle
or rooms of metal-worked jars—dowries

she might have saved for children instead of sold
to antique shops, had they not wanted to go
somewhere else too, away from there,

to reinvent themselves as engineers or doctors
after university. I wanted to sketch them, lay
bands of brilliant color beside each other

and beside the bleached starkness of coiled
snake bone, another ornament the locals
traditionally wore in their hair. As I took

photographs, our host asked if I might like
to pose for a picture in the manner of native women
in the old days: plaited hair, wrap skirt; nothing

except beads around my neck, massed
artfully and arranged upon my breasts. I knew
about the portraits of Masferré, those girls

with regal foreheads and nubile breasts
balancing tiers of clay pots on their dark heads,
rippled tattoos visible at the edges of brass

bracelets and boar's tooth amulets. And yet,
I am a bit ashamed to admit in recollection,
I refused—concerned about modesty,

blushing at the thought of being peeled back
to only this layer of skin. If I knew then what I
know now, which is of course to say I realize

a self is so much more than the sum of molting
skins, more than an idea of remainders after
what one thinks has been given and spent

or taken away—I might have said yes; I might
have proof the future held forgiving shapes—seed
after seed to perforate at the center of each stone.

YOLO

On the second to the last day of my visit,
my octogenarian mother comes to my hotel room
bearing two slightly dented cardboard boxes.
From the tissue folds of one, she pulls out

shoes bought from the market or the mall—
one of those places overrun with cheap goods
from China, screaming *Fashionista!* or *New Trend!*
For you, she says, displaying a pair of High

Top sneakers. She dangles them under the light,
presumably so I might better admire layer
on layer of ruffled yellow gold lace applied
where there should have been serviceable

canvas—*You can wear this going to the grocery;*
or even when you garden. I look at her but there is
no trace of irony in her voice: she is completely serious.
Too bright, not my taste (the unvoiced *Are you kidding me?*)—

my spluttering protests that she dismisses with a gnarled
wave of the hand, at least two fingers adorned with a gem-
encrusted ring. Their sparkle (costume? real? I cannot tell)
cuts the air as she continues with her campaign: *Try, try!*

And I must oblige her as I did throughout my girlhood,
all those times I let her dress me in frocks she'd sewn
by hand, lace-edged socks and matching shoes she picked out
when we went to Gregg's and she spent a good hour or more

trying calfskin pumps or buckled T-straps, admiring
how three-inch heels set off her shapely calves.
Regarding the High Tops: they fit, if a little snugly
at the toe. Justified, I hold my ground, saying

they wouldn't allow room for socks. Miffed, she drops them
back into their box, saying she bought them for herself first,
anyway—The last word, still hers. I sigh, bracing for
the contents of the second box, which now she opens

triumphantly: *Maybe this one!* It's a pair of deep
pink ballerina flats, fake microsuede, each with a tuft
or pompom resembling an uncombed head or sea
anemone. Before I slip my feet into them

I already know these are the ones I'll need to pack
in my luggage: a kind of truce though there has been
no real conflict waged, as if my place in the cosmic order
can now be reinstated even if it was never taken away.

There's one more surprise: *YOLO,* she says, *You Only
Live Once*—It comes out so fast I'm not sure
that I've heard right. But she says it again, she urges
me to wear them on my feet *now, this instant*—as if

to wait another second would drain them of their vivid
hue, as if the hesitation might line each flimsy sole
with leaden weights and going, I'd never again feel
borne by merely an earth-bound current.

Five Remedies for Sadness

Aquinas suggests five remedies for when the fizz
bottoms out of the champagne, for when the balloon tied to the body

can't even lever a dust mote to save the day—Not: Wallow in ballads from the jukebox,
dance with one arm wrapped around your neck, the other your shoulder. Not: swallow

every cachou that smells faintly of burnt almonds. He is firm and eschews improv:
first, he says, grant yourself something you like—And yes, I like the idea of a bateau

going by the name *Pleasure* bobbing on the surface of the oily water, ready to punt
headfirst toward somewhere other than here. Second, assuage your sorrows

in the form of weeping. Have a good cry, find some little refreshment in catharsis, for
just as laughter does not take away from joy, tears do not damage sorrow. In a souq,

keepsakes are sold: tear catchers of glass tipped with bronze or silver, spindles to keep
lachrimae harvested from each eye. I'll bring back just one each for you, my daughters—no

more than that. Something to show by way of novelty to your friends, yes? & your gremlin? Next, contemplate the truth of your sadness: its peculiar song inducing earworm,

or when it coincides with cravings for chocolate and chips, according to your journal. Patchouli's next; or a peppermint scrub, followed by naps on the couch or hammock.

Quell sadness by bathing and sleeping, is his final note. That's right, no J(k). Reviewed, remixed, his remedies read a bit like New Age—not medieval—wisdom. I

sag sometimes beneath the peculiar sorrow of being the hotline daughters turn to when each tangos with her own demons. Then I get FaceTime and phone calls frantic with sobbing,

urgent pleas for help. Thomas, what else can you tell me of sorrow branching from sorrow? Of visceral pains that tear me up, head-heart-psyche, because of my mother-nature?

When finally I fall into sleep (after a hot bath, as prescribed), xylems pull from the roots of old fears and swell with pressure. *Pane*, panic—

yeasts from similar spores? O to starve forever what feeds on the bread of misgiving. Rhumb zeroing in on the mother of cures for malaise: just not enough to numb, and not yet nirvana.

Dream Landscape at the Edge of This World

> *"As flies to wanton boys are we to th' gods,*
> *They kill us for their sport."*
>
> ~ *Shakespeare,* King Lear, *act 4, scene 1*

What to make of a dream in which
fields are littered with decapitated
remains, the sightless heads of the fallen
in even rows tilted up at the sky, their hair
matted with dried blood yet somehow
artfully arranged like fringes of grotesque
sunflowers? What to make of the pair of us,
winding hand in hand through grounds
made slick with the issue from these bodies,
the air rank and thick with flies? You were
frailer than I ever remembered, slight
in a thin cotton wrapper, undone by
the terrible waste surrounding us. I led
as if now the parent and you the child,
feeling as if somehow I'd been there before,
winding through maze-like paths flanked
by hedges made of reeds whose ends
were quilled blades. Ahead, an armored
shape emerged from out of its cave; I stayed
our progress, trembling in the crosshatches.
What might we do if we had plumes or wings?
And yet on every side, the puce from doves'
breasts dripped warnings on the rocks. Bent low
to the ground, at last we found our way to where
a dying sentinel stood guard at the edge of this
world: he dipped his finger in his blood and marked
our heads; then pointed out the exit in the distance.

Lying here in the darkness,
I let the days obliterate me

I let the rooms empty
themselves of their contents
a little more each day and fill
my hands with perfume from peeled
oranges, with residues of salt. The great
harp that twanged in the summer gardens
has long ceased vibrating. Rain fills
the cisterns to the brim. All that has cause
to happen is happening. It is impossible
to turn back the clocks, to give the dead
bird its blasted wing. Why not start
anywhere and make that the beginning.
Why not keep going through
the numbered pages. Why not address
that letter to eternity; why not come back
and pick up where you left off
the last time you were here.

~ *after Borges*

Calling the Soul Back to the Body

It swings imperceptibly on the slack
end of a clothesline. Dark hooded shape,

wings glossier than tree ear mushrooms, its
marble eye fixed on my own. Every afternoon

I come to the kitchen threshold
and there it sits; I almost want to raise

my right hand and swear with my left
on the cover of a sacred book. It never stays

long—swooping into the bush to stab
a worm in half before arcing away

into the sky. Vines settle back upon
their blue-green cowl when it leaves.

Say to the soul, I know you. Chant a spell
learned long ago: *Maykan, maykan, di ka agbutbuteng.*

Come back, come back, do not be frightened. [Ilocano]

ACKNOWLEDGMENTS

Thank you to poet and publisher Dave Bonta, my co-blogger at *Via Negativa* (www.vianegativa.us), where I have written at least a poem a day since November 20, 2010; as well as to the editors and staff of the following publications where these poems first appeared, sometimes in different forms and under different titles:

Orion, Spring 2020
  "Where the Seed Scattered"
A Dozen Nothing, September 2019
  "Elegy for Loss"
  "Fatalism"
  "Hibernal"
  "Texture of the Lost"
  "Theory of Instruction"
  "When I Think I Could Be Beautiful"
Aesthetica Magazine (UK), December 2015
  "In the hotel with thin walls and the name of a poet"

I am indebted to Allison Joseph and Jon Tribble for their faith in these poems; to the Crab Orchard Series in Poetry; and to Southern Illinois University Press, Kristine Priddy, and Wayne Larsen for the care that went into the production of this book. So much gratitude to Lilledeshan Bose and the estate of Santiago Bose for permission to use the book cover image; there could not have been any other. Thank you to the writers and friends and my students over the years, too numerous to name, who give so much inspiration and strength from the beauty of their stories and words. Finally, to my families here and on the other side of the water for their love and unwavering support.

Other Books in the Crab Orchard Series in Poetry